Anxiety

Put An End To Your Constant Worrying And Stress By Stopping Your Internal Monologue And Thinking Less

(The All In One Solution To Overcome Anxiety)

Polyvios Liakos

TABLE OF CONTENT

Isolation Of Oneself As A Direct Result Of Anxiety 1

How To Carry Out A Smart Breakdown For Your Weekly Objectives 6

The Pathway Of The Amygdala 14

How To Boost Your Current Income Right Now 26

Experience-Based Counseling And Therapy (Act) 35

How Exactly Does Music Therapy Help People Who Are Depressed? 51

A General Synopsis Of Our Opinions 66

Feelings Of Happiness And A Healthy Body Go Hand In Hand. 78

How To Conquer Anxiety And Live Your Life To The Fullest 86

Developing Your Own Self-Assurance While Engaging In Conversation 97

Gratitude And Acknowledgment 106

Putting Yourself Out There And Seeking Assistance Along With Surrounding Yourself With Support 114

Methods To Either Completely Eliminate Or Significantly Reduce Anxiety 116

The Application Of Thought Journals To Disorders Of Social Anxiety 133

Isolation Of Oneself As A Direct Result Of Anxiety

The person who is pushed to become codependent in a relationship is the exact opposite of the person who gets avoidant in those same connections. When you're in a relationship with someone, you need to be willing to expose yourself emotionally and be open to the other person's feelings, despite the fact that there's always a chance that you could end up getting wounded. There is no assurance that any relationship will continue on for the rest of one's life. Because of this, being in a relationship always comes with the possibility of getting injured. What happens, therefore, if your anxiety about being wounded in a relationship is so great that you end up simply avoiding emotional involvement at all costs?

Being away from a location is not the only component of self-isolation. Relationships with persons who are emotionally unavailable are among the most challenging kinds of connections to maintain. It is not unheard of for a person to be married to another person for a number of years and yet have no idea how that person feels about them. This occurs frequently due to the fact that unhealthy attachment can also emerge as self-isolation or an inability to emotionally open up to others.

Let's go back to the child who endured a troubled upbringing for a moment. They probably never heard anything but negative comments from either of their parents. They probably did not receive enough affection and probably did not have somebody to whom they could truly express their feelings. This child will eventually turn inside and learn to disconnect and detach from other people as their condition worsens. As a toddler, it is only natural that they are unable to physically leave things; therefore, the only alternative is for them to emotionally pack up and leave. As soon as this characteristic gets engrained in them, they will have a difficult time emotionally opening up, even when they are an adult.

Fear of being injured by other people is the primary motivator for self-isolation. You start to feel anxious about the prospect of being wounded if you allow yourself to be vulnerable or open up to others. This indicates that even when you are in a relationship, you will keep your guard up since, at the end of the day, all you are trying to do is protect yourself from experiencing pain. You may believe that by doing this, you are protecting yourself from experiencing heartbreak; nevertheless, in most cases, you wind up missing out on opportunities to form connections that are both healthy and important.

It is far more difficult for individuals to form an emotional connection with you when they are unable to comprehend the emotions that you are experiencing. The connection starts to feel cold, and your spouse starts looking for emotional connections with others outside of the partnership. If you allow worry and the fear of being vulnerable to control the way you think and behave, the end effect will be that you will feel lonely even when you are surrounded by other people.

It is quite challenging to have a healthy connection when you are unable to be vulnerable with other people. People will make an effort to comprehend you, but they will be driven away by the barriers that you have built around yourself in order to protect yourself. The problem with worry is that rather than giving you control over the situation, it strips you of the ability to think and behave in a reasonable manner. Fear can be a powerful motivator, but the vast majority of the things we do when we are terrified are never productive and, in the vast majority of circumstances, will only take you down the path to your own ruin.

How To Carry Out A Smart Breakdown For Your Weekly Objectives

An example of a SMART breakdown based on the goals discussed previously.

Specific to the First Week: In an effort to reduce the negative effects of my anxiety, I plan to practice meditation and deep breathing techniques on a regular basis.

Measurable goal: In order to better manage my anxiety, I plan to devote five minutes of each day to practicing meditation and deep breathing techniques.

Attainable - I am able to carve out five minutes out of my day, even if I have to create the time for it, in order to complete the meditation and breathing exercises.

Relevant: Both breathing exercises and meditation will assist me in relaxing my body, which will in turn assist me in lowering my stress levels, which will help with my anxiety.

Regarding the passage of time, my goal is to be able to meditate or do breathing exercises for five minutes each day by the end of the first week.

Result (using positive statements): I was able to achieve this objective four out of the seven days. I shall begin week one once more, and I am confident that this time I will have even greater success. On the days when I remembered to do the task, I did experience a reduction in the amount of anxiety that I was feeling.

Specific to Week Two: I want to meditate more frequently every day and start include some light exercise in my daily routine in order to help minimize the amount of anxiety I have.

I want to start meditating every day for ten minutes, and I also want to start doing some mild exercise for five to ten minutes. I want my goals to be measurable.

Attainable: I have successfully finished the first week, and I am certain that I will be able to locate a total of twenty minutes in each day that I can commit to taking care of myself and my health.

Relevant: Not only will meditating assist me in lowering my levels of tension and anxiety, but also engaging in some mild physical activity will assist me in lowering my levels of stress and anxiety while simultaneously boosting my confidence in myself.

Time-Related: I would consider it a success if I could accomplish all of these objectives within the next week.

The end result is that I was able to do what I set out to do this week, and I am now prepared to go on to the third week. I'm starting to get a better sense of who I am, and it's helping me become more optimistic about myself. My anxiety is at its lowest point in months, possibly even longer.

Specific to Week Three: I want to begin meditating each day, even more so than before, and I also want to keep up with my workout routine. I would like to begin eating more healthfully.

Measurable: I would like to begin meditating every day for fifteen minutes and increase the amount of gentle exercise I do each day to ten minutes. Breakfast and lunch are the meals of the day in which I wish to find healthier options.

Attainable - Given how quickly we moved into week two, I get the impression that switching to a healthy diet won't be that much of a challenge for me. If I keep pushing myself, I am confident that I will reach my goals.

Relevant: The next step in working on myself and devoting time to myself is to incorporate a healthy diet in addition to all of the other actions I have made to lessen the stress and worry.

Time-Related: I will give myself seven days to fulfill this objective; however, because I am adding other objectives that are more difficult, I am aware that it is possible that I will have to start again with week three. I have come to terms with the fact that addressing my anxiety will not always be simple.

The outcome is going to be that I will have to repeat week three, which is something that I had previously prepared myself for as a possibility. I was able to successfully have a better breakfast, but it was much simpler for me to grab something unhealthy for lunch than it was to go through the drive-thru. I did experience quite a few failures throughout this first week, but I am optimistic that I will be able to get back on track with my objectives if I simply repeat this week.

Specific to Week Four: I want to increase the amount of time I spend meditating and keep up my light workout routine. My goal is to eat well-balanced meals at least thrice a day.

Measurable: I want to raise the amount of time I spend meditating to twenty minutes per day, I want to increase the amount of time I spend doing mild exercise to ten minutes per day, and I want to ensure that I eat three meals per day that are healthy and encourage a healthier lifestyle.

Attainable - I have finally finished week three, which put me behind schedule, but I have been able to meditate for fifteen minutes, exercise consistently for seven minutes, and prepare two meals a day that are completely nutritious and healthful. I am certain that I will be able to surpass these objectives.

Relevant: Because I have already begun to observe the effects of the adjustments I have made to my lifestyle and food, I am aware that increasing the number of times I implement these changes and eating healthily at all times will enhance the effects. My self-assurance has already begun to reach new heights, and this will undoubtedly assist me in reaching my goals in that regard.

Because this is the final week of the short-term goals I have set for myself, I am aware that it is possible that I may not be able to accomplish all of these things in the week that I have allotted to myself. I'm going to give myself a week to see whether I can accomplish them.

The final result is that, after seven days, I have decided to make this week longer than it was originally scheduled to be. I am making good progress toward accomplishing this objective; nonetheless, I would like to focus on developing a timetable that incorporates it. My stress level has decreased, my anxiety level has decreased, and my confidence level has skyrocketed!

It is now up to you to act. You are free to utilize any number of copies that are required. Writing things down several times can sometimes aid with memorizing and also boosts confidence.

The Pathway Of The Amygdala

The amygdala is a component of the route that comes next. In spite of the fact that the cortex pathway to anxiety may seem more easily identifiable or justifiable due to the fact that we are frequently conscious of the thoughts that it generates, the amygdala is the region of the brain that is responsible for the initial stages of the physical feeling of worry. Because of its central location and connections across the brain, it is able to exert control over the release of hormones and activate the parts of the brain that are responsible for the physical manifestations of anxiety. In the here and now, the amygdala has groundbreaking and instantaneous effects on the body, and they are critically important to comprehend.

The Amygdala is involved.

The amygdala is positioned in close proximity to the center of the cerebral cortex. However, it is customary to refer to the amygdala as one thing, so we will continue with this training even though the brain actually has two amygdalae, one in the left hemisphere and one in the right. As was just mentioned, one is located in the left hemisphere, and the other is located in the right. You can determine where your right amygdala is located by pointing your left forefinger at your right eye and your right pointer into your right ear canal. This will help you pinpoint its precise location. Converging the lines from your two fingers reveals the location of the right amygdala, which is the goal of this convergence. Because of its characteristic almond form, the structure known as the amygdala got its name from the Greek word for almond. The amygdala stores a significant number of our emotional responses, both good and negative. These responses can be either pleasant or unpleasant. When someone invades your personal space or gets in your face, the amygdala is the part of your brain that is responsible for the rage you experience. On the other hand, if you meet somebody who reminds you of your grandmother and you have a warm notion of liking for this woman you don't know anything about, that is also the amygdala, and it is currently a charming emotional memory. The amygdala examines memories of past feelings, and if you have a healthy amygdala, your own emotional reactions will most likely strike you as being positive.

The Lateral Nucleus of the Cell

The amygdala is partitioned into a few distinct regions; however, the focus of this article will be primarily on two of these regions, both of which play important roles in the formation of emotional responses such as fear and anxiety. The part of the amygdala that is responsible for receiving incoming messages from the faculties is called the lateral nucleus. It is always processing your experiences and is primed and ready to respond to any indication of danger that may arise. Its job, much like that of a built-in alarm system, is to identify any potential threat that you perceive, whether it be through sight, sound, smell, or touch, and then to signal its presence. The information that it needs comes from the thalamus. The truth is that it receives information before the cortex does, and it is extremely important to keep this fact in mind.

The amygdala pathway is the more direct route from our faculties to the lateral nucleus, which is one of the reasons why information can be sent there so quickly. The amygdala is hardwired to respond quickly enough to protect your life in dangerous situations. According to research done by Armony et al. in 1995, a simple pathway inside the brain's wiring makes it possible for information to get quickly to the lateral nucleus of the amygdala, which enables the brain to have a rapid response. When information is received by our sense organs, such as our eyes, hearing, nose, or fingertips, it is sent from those organs to the thalamus, and then the thalamus transfers this information directly to the amygdala. During this time, the information is also being transmitted to the amygdala from the thalamus. At the same time, the thalamus is also responsible for relaying information to the appropriate regions of the cortex so that it can be processed at a higher level. Regardless of this fact, the amygdala is the first part of the brain to receive new information before it can be processed by the other lobes of the cortex. This suggests that the lateral nucleus of the amygdala can react to protect you from danger before the cortex even recognizes what the potential danger is.

The amygdala receives information from the thalamus, which enables it to react even before the cortex has a chance to process the information and conceive of a response. Despite the fact that this may seem you as peculiar, if you think back on your own experiences, you can almost certainly recall a few instances in which something similar took place. Have you ever been in a situation in which you had to respond intuitively before you had the opportunity to understand what you were responding to?

Consider the case of Melinda, a young girl of 10 years old who was looking for camping equipment in the basement of her house. She took a few steps through the doorway before retracing her steps out of terror. The sight of a coat hanging securely on a coatrack was the impetus for her reaction. Her amygdala had a reaction to the condition of the coat, which could have been an intruder, and it caused her to leap a great distance away from the "trespasser" before she even realized what it was that she had seen. The amygdala is hardwired to react before the cortex can as a protective strategy built into the brain during development.

The cortex, which is concerned mostly with big picture issues, makes more effort to comprehend information coming from the thalamus. In the case of Melinda, the visual information should be transmitted to the occipital projection at the back of the brain. From there, it should be transmitted to the frontal lobes, which are the regions where the information is integrated and where educated decisions are made. That is the reason why Melinda sprang back so quickly, but she recovered in a moment and continued searching for the outdoor hardware: it halted for a second for her cortex to convey the information that the dark shape was a completely innocuous coat. Melinda recovered in a moment and continued her search.

To work out:

Humming softly to yourself with your mouth and eyes closed for the next five minutes. In the pauses, make sure to take several deep breaths. You can carry out this exercise in a variety of positions, including kneeling, standing, or sitting with your back in a straight line.

This activity can seem like a waste of time, but there is a lot that can be gleaned by listening to the sound of one's own voice while humming for a long period of time. The sound of humming has a calming effect on both the body and the mind, much like the sound of falling rain, crickets in the evening, the rustle of leaves, or a waterfall. It is thought that the wavelengths that are produced and sent out in a continuous flow are responsible for this impact of relaxation.

However, the fact that it is closely connected to your breathing is maybe the most fascinating aspect of your humming. If you take shallow, hurried breaths, your hum will not be as lengthy or as effective. On the other hand, if you take focused, deep breaths, your hum will serve to relax your body and maybe bring you into the here and now. Have you taken any notice of the fact that you were the one who was relaxing you? You did not require the presence of any other person or thing in order to achieve a state of peace and stillness.

Humming to oneself and tuning in to the waves that you generate within your own being is a healthy practice that should be done sometimes. This is something that is constantly accessible to you in the here and now.

*Ten minutes of stillness during which you focus on your breath. Mantra: "Calmness and stillness are always present." Repeat this mantra as often as possible.

(If you want to share this experience, use the hashtag #30DAYSHUM.)

Day 10

To work out:

Find something that you are able to smash, whether it be an egg, a drinking glass, a pencil, or anything else. You should only shatter the item of your choice in a secure location, and you should exercise extra caution if it is made of glass or is otherwise sharp.

Rather of immediately cleaning up the mess, you should examine it and then let the pieces sit for at least a few minutes before cleaning them.

Were you the one who broke the object, or did I break it by telling you to break it? And if you think that you were the only person who broke the object, then ask yourself this: Did the object let you break it? This is not an activity designed to help relieve feelings of annoyance or tension. This lesson's objective is to demonstrate to you that you are not entirely responsible for the perceived disorder, disarray, loss, or shattered parts in your life.

The act of destroying something in the here and now is perfectly acceptable. We spend a great deal of time worrying about things like our objectives, plans, relationships, jobs, circumstances, and the future, amongst other things, falling apart. And when something like this occurs, we have a tendency to blame ourselves or others since that is how we were brought up to react. Allow the object to shatter and examine both the bits it creates and your own reaction to the breakdown of the object.

*Ten minutes of stillness during which you focus on your breath. The mantra should be repeated as often as possible: "I cannot harm or break the present moment."

How To Boost Your Current Income Right Now

Your current income may be increased in a variety of ways, and I am going to show you how to achieve that in this chapter. However, you need to be willing to follow my directions as I guide you toward achieving your objectives. The methods that I will teach you are very straightforward and practical, and they are certain to be successful. Even though there are a lot of different methods that you may bring in more money, the easiest one is to simply ask your boss or whoever it is that you work for for a raise as soon as you see them. This should be done whenever you have the opportunity. Do not wait for the right time since there is a possibility that there will never be the right time. Even though many people would advise against asking him while he is in a bad mood, I advise you to ask him anyhow. The reason that I recommend that you do it despite the fact that he is not in the most upbeat frame of mind is because taking action on him when he is in that state of mind sends him a message that you are not afraid of him firing you or of his mood; instead, it demonstrates boldness and that it is urgent for him to take action upon your request. I suggest that you do this even though he is not in the most upbeat frame of mind. Because they are equally concerned about losing skilled workers.

How do I go about asking him for a pay raise?

In Order to take such action first you must write it down on a piece of paper rehearse in front of the mirror as if you were sitting in front of him and sell yourself as best as possible to him, letting him or her know how valuable you are to the company, you must let him know for example how long its been since he gave you a raise, remember he does not really care about your problems but he does care about the company and remember he can get fired just like you. Therefore, you need to portray yourself to the firm as a valued asset that the company can benefit from. You will need to devise strategies to accomplish it. You must let him know that you are a dependable worker and that you are always capable of completing any task that is handed to you, that you never miss work and that you are never late, and how he can count on you in anything that is related to work. You should also mention how long you have worked for the company; it does not matter if it has only been three months; you can inquire that in those three months you have learned a lot, been responsible, and that you have demonstrated your value to the company. If he does decide to grant you a raise, you are obligated to inquire as to when the rise will take effect. in order to avoid having to wait for several months because their duty is to keep the costs as low as they may be.

What are the repercussions in the event that they refuse?

If he decides not to offer you a raise, you should not become irate or troublesome because this will ultimately work out in your advantage. Because they are unable to provide you the rise that you requested from them today, you are now able to recognize that the company is not a good fit for you to work for and that you should go elsewhere for employment opportunities. I advise you find a different employer to work for immediately. I propose you aim high; it doesn't matter if you have no experience in a new industry as long as you have the will that can be your best advantage. Many people would advice that you insist on asking until your boss can no longer refuse. I suggest that you find a different employer to work for immediately. Some jobs will require you to obtain a certificate or some sort of formal education, while others may not. Why would you compete in a profession where you are at a disadvantage if you already have certificates in the career that you have chosen because that is your area of strength? If you do have certifications, you must focus on the career that you have chosen because that is your area of strength. If you do not own any certifications, you need to concentrate on finding jobs that do not require those items. Believe it or not, there are professions that pay well but do not require these certificates. In point of fact, just as in other places, they will teach you all it is necessary for you to know while you are there.

When looking for a career that pays higher, you need to be persistent and locate something that you believe you would enjoy doing at the same time. You could even be turned down multiple times before they decide to hire you, but you can rest assured that if they see you applying for the same position multiple times, they will hire you. The narrative of a motivational speaker by the name of Less Brown, who talks about how he got a job as a radio broadcaster without any experience and how he was denied multiple times before the management got tired of him pestering him for a job that he just hired him, is both incredibly inspiring and humorous at the same time. Less Brown's story is a great example of how anyone can achieve their goals despite the challenges they face. The funniest part is that it actually worked for me. During this time, you are required to speak only with the person in charge of hiring, as he is the one who will decide whether or not to accept your application. If you are successful in getting the job, you will then be required to explain the reasons behind your decision to leave your previous employer. I would recommend that you explain to him that you are looking for a better opportunity and a better work environment and that the company you are applying for seems to fulfill all of your needs, that the company looks like a good company to work for, and that you have heard great things about it in the past months upon doing your research, but you should only explain it in that form because in that form, you are making him feel good about his company and you are basically letting him know that he has done a good job with the company

After you have accomplished this goal, you are to have a conversation about money and how much you anticipate getting paid. You are required to make a request for pay that is an increment of three or four dollars higher than what your salary is at the time. When he says that, you should immediately ask when and how much, so that he knows you are expecting that extra dollar in the time he has appointed, then when the time has arrived, you must remind him about it because they might forget or try to keep you at the lower pay for as long as possible. He will either decline your request or suggest a lower pay to start and promise you perhaps another dollar in a given amount of time. If he declines your request, he will suggest a lower pay to start. You may need to do this an innumerable number of times, but always keep in mind that "you miss every shot you don't take." Therefore, my advice is that you fire more frequently rather than not at all.

Experience-Based Counseling And Therapy (Act)

The acronym "ACT" stands for acceptance and commitment therapy, which is an innovative form of cognitive behavioral therapy (CBT) that has received a great deal of attention in recent years. It places an emphasis on helping people overcome the challenges of life by embracing their values, accepting themselves as they are, and practicing mindfulness.

ACT is predicated on the idea that human suffering is an inherent and unavoidable component of being human, and this idea serves as one of its primary assumptions. It also revolves around people's attempts to take control of their own experiences or steer clear of situations that could result in human suffering and other aspects of our life that are not functioning properly. People who want to learn how to effectively manage their pain, practice mindfulness, get clarity on what aspects of their lives are most important, and search for a life that has more meaning can benefit from ACT. The purpose of acceptance and commitment therapy (ACT) is not to eliminate suffering; rather, it aims to teach people how to go through life with a minimum of stress and difficulty.

Because its researchers and practitioners are dedicated to the advancement of science and the empirical investigation of its origins and effects, acceptance and commitment therapy (ACT) is recognized as an empirical kind of psychotherapy.

As of the year 2014, the ACT had been the focus of investigation in more than 80 randomized clinical trials for a variety of problems, including a total of over 5,000 participants. This type of cognitive behavioral therapy has also been used to design a non-therapeutic version of the same processes called as Acceptance and Commitment Training. This training is centered on the development of values skills, acceptance, and mindfulness, and it was created using this form of CBT.

The Relational Frame Approach to Theory

The foundational idea of activity-based learning (ACT) is called the Relational Frame Theory (RFT). The purpose of RFT is to investigate the relationship between human behavior and language.

The ability to comprehend language is essential for successful psychotherapy. A good many of us make use of language both internally, when we are thinking, and externally, when we are communicating with the people in our immediate environment. We think about, read about, write about, talk about, assess, relate, categorize, and characterize everything that is going on around us using language.

Language is an important component of our life as human beings; without it, it is possible that we would not have had the opportunity to develop our civilizations.

For instance, we would be unable to create laws and other societal regulations to govern our behavior if we did not have language.

Although there are many advantages to human language, there is also the possibility that it has certain disadvantages. It is comparable to the yin and yang, as it possesses both a potent dark side as well as a potent bright side. According to RFT, language also plays a significant part in the anguish that humans experience. Language is a tool that we use to construct negative thoughts, obsess over things, and rehash experiences that caused us distress in the past. We also use language to form prejudiced and hostile judgments about others in our immediate environment. Excessive use of language and thought may also make it difficult to remain in touch with the here and now. It is possible for us to lose the ability to enjoy the here and now if we allow ourselves to become preoccupied with thoughts of the past and the uncertainties of the future.

By gaining a more in-depth understanding of human language and the mechanism behind it, we can better harness the positive aspects of language in order to reduce the negative impacts of its use. This is the kind of comprehension that RFT hopes to convey to its audience with the help of ACT.

The study of how human language affects our conduct typically focuses on two outstanding elements of language: generativities and symbolism. Psychotherapists who are investigating how human language affects our behavior typically concentrate on these two aspects of language.

Because language is employed to allude to a thing or a concept, symbolism is not difficult to comprehend at all. For instance, a "tree" is a form of plant that has a trunk that supports branches and leaves and may or may not contain flowers or fruits. The word "tree" refers to this sort of plant. Things can be symbolically expressed through the use of language. When you have a better knowledge of a certain term, you will then be able to comprehend the meaning of that word.

On the other hand, the term "generativity" alludes to our capacity to generate and comprehend an infinite number of meaningful statements. Productivity is another name for this concept. Every language is comprised of a predetermined quantity of fundamental letters, sounds, and words. On the other hand, each one of us is capable of producing an infinite number of phrases that are completely original by using these words, letters, and sounds.

There have been many different theories produced to investigate these characteristics; typically, these theories identify the essential qualities or focus on a variety of topics. Linguists, for example, are of the opinion that genetic elements are primarily responsible for the originality, complexity, and generativity of language. Cognitive psychologists are of the opinion that our brain is responsible for the way in which we process and store information, including symbolisms.

In spite of the fact that they focus on different aspects of language, the vast majority of studies of language are founded on the concept that language is used to express information that is generated by our brains. Language is, at its core, a system of symbols that allows us to communicate our thoughts in a way that can be comprehended by other others. These theories frequently center their attention on linguistic phenomena that are seen as being of fundamental significance.

RFT researchers and practitioners use a different approach to investigate language and cognition than traditional researchers and practitioners. RFT focuses on how humans acquire language through contact with other people and their environment rather than explaining language as a means of transferring ideas from one person to another. This is not simply a description of the idea; rather, it is structured to provide a meaningful and practical examination of language as well as cognition.

Because it works with individuals to assist them in employing language as a means of resolving certain psychological disorders, ACT is often referred to as the applied technology of RFT. This is something that can be accomplished through the use of the distinctive ACT model of psychological flexibility.

a model based on psychological adaptability and flexibility

The primary purpose of engaging in ACT is to improve one's psychological flexibility. This refers to one's ability to maintain contact with the now and now as a fully conscious human being while, depending on the demands of the situation, either remaining consistent in one's behavior or altering that behavior in order to better serve one's chosen ideals.

To put this in more layman's terms, this indicates that we should treat our own feelings and thoughts with a bit more tolerance and base our actions on our long-term values rather than our fleeting emotions, thoughts, and impulses.

This is a possibility due to the fact that thoughts and feelings have a history of being unreliable markers of long-term values. They are difficult to keep under control, and they have a propensity to act in an extreme manner. When we always let our ideas and emotions to dictate our behavior, we run the risk of missing the more significant, rising patterns of action, and we also run the risk of failing to comprehend the actual significance in our lives or experiencing the richness that life has to offer.

At the moment, psychological flexibility is evaluated with the help of a tool called the Acceptance and Action Questionnaire. This tool is utilized by psychotherapists and ACT specialists, and it is used to make predictions about the following psychological concerns:

Depressive state

Unsatisfactory performance on the job

Misuse of substances

a susceptibility to anxiety

Long-term incapacity or inability

A higher level of anxiousness

Pathology in a general sense

Ithymia Alexithymia

Worry

The development of psychological adaptability can be accomplished through the application of six core ACT processes. It is important to keep in mind that each procedure is viewed as a beneficial psychological skill, and not as a specialized method for resolving psychological difficulties.

10. Take in some musical sounds

It is astounding to think that music has the ability to calm an anxious mind.

A number of studies have indicated that music with a calming effect has a significant and beneficial effect on the human emotions.

Instrumental music has proven to be the most effective form of music for alleviating stress. Why? Because listening to songs with lyrics compels the brain to come up with an explanation for what's being said. As a direct consequence of this, the capacity of the brain to relax will be impaired.

Keeping stress under control might be difficult at times. The majority of people are powerless to escape a stressful situation because they are ill-equipped to deal with it. However, as a result of the never-ending efforts of scientific research, there are now viable options. There is no need to go out and get any kind of medication for your stress.

For example, a recent study discovered a brand new approach to get rid of stress immediately. This procedure is both speedy and uncomplicated. You will only require a sheet of paper and a pen to complete this task. It was discovered that music therapy is an excellent method for lowering depressive symptoms in adolescents. It is also beneficial to one's self-esteem. The prior study, which included more than two hundred people, served as the basis for the finding.

The researchers ended up splitting the subjects into two different groups. While one group participated in music therapy, the other functioned as a control group throughout the experiment. During the course of the experiment, the researchers questioned the participants about how they felt when playing a certain track.

The participants who were given the therapy had reduced levels of depression and higher levels of self-esteem, according to the findings of the study. This study has the potential to be of great assistance in the treatment of young people who have behavioral issues. Additionally, it can direct specialists on the appropriate course of action to take. Professor Sam Porter, who was the principal investigator of the study, provided his major findings.

"The findings that are contained in our report should be considered by healthcare providers and commissioners when making decisions about the sort of care for young people that they wish to support," added Porter.

The practice of treating patients with music has been around for at least a thousand years. Music was really used as a form of healing by the ancient Greek philosophers. People who were diagnosed with depression were given the recommendation to listen to the soothing music of a flute. On the other hand, the formal music therapy techniques didn't start until the 1940s in the contemporary age. After the end of World War II, mental health experts began using music therapy on veterans suffering from post-traumatic stress disorder (PTSD).

Musicians travel to mental hospitals to play music for veterans suffering from post-traumatic stress disorder (PTSD). Since that time, professionals in the medical field have begun to recognize the benefits of music therapy.

Every day, each of us deals with something that might be considered stressful. It could be your supervisor at work, your responsibilities at school, or even your romantic life. It doesn't matter how hard we try to steer clear of unfavorable situations, it always seems like they find a way to find us.

As a result, when we are under pressure, we have a tendency to look for answers. When it comes to relieving emotional strain, the most comprehensive source of information is found on the internet. There are thousands of different strategies and methods available to alleviate anxiety.

However, not all of those strategies are available for no cost and are supported by scientific evidence. However, in the following section of the book, I am going to discuss with you one of the remarkable findings that was obtained from scientific research. Everyone who is looking for a way to unwind will, without a shadow of a doubt, find this to be of tremendous assistance. This method of relieving stress is completely free, and it does not require any specific amount of time or space to be effective.

One song in particular is the strategy that I'm going to talk about. A song that, when played, can lessen feelings of anxiety by as much as 65% in its listeners. The name of this product is "Weightless" and it was created by Marconi Union.

In the course of his work at Mindlab International, Dr. David Lewis-Hodgson undertook a study to analyze the songs that have the ability to help people relax.

Participants in the study were given the task of solving puzzles as part of the protocol. In order to accomplish this goal, the activity was designed to be somewhat stressful. The participants were not only working on the task at hand, but they were also listening to a variety of music as the researchers assessed several aspects of their physiology, including their heart rate, blood pressure, and respiration. According to the findings, playing the song "Weightless" in its entirety can lower anxiety by as much as 65 percent.

Marconi Union, with the assistance of a number of different sound therapists, purposefully composed the music "Weightless" and released it. The harmony, rhythms, and bass were all meticulously tuned to induce a state of relaxation in the audience.

The prior study provides proof that listening to music has a positive impact on the health of humans. It's possible that this is the reason why our predecessors have always had such a deep appreciation for music. They were joyful and healthy as a result of the music.

How Exactly Does Music Therapy Help People Who Are Depressed?

The treatment takes into account a person's physiological, emotional, and social requirements. People are able to convey their feelings and thoughts without having to use their mouths when they create music or listen to music created by others. A person's heart rate, breathing rate, and other types of physical activity could be slowed down by the combination of melody, rhythm, and melody. The action causes an increase in the amount of dopamine that is secreted in the brain, which, in turn, makes the individual feel happier.

The Repetitive Loop Consisting of Thoughts, Feelings, and Actions

This takes place as a direct result of the cyclical nature of human activity. Your thoughts have an effect on your feelings, which in turn have an effect on the activities you engage in. This is something that is well acknowledged within the field of psychology in general and is something that can be grasped with relative ease. The way in which you understand the environment around you is strongly tied to the thoughts that you have. The majority of them are founded on the judgments that you form unconsciously as you go through life and interact with the world. The more you encounter something without questioning it, the more your subconscious mind will come to accept it without your conscious mind's interference. Your subconscious is aware that you are making a silent agreement by not correcting yourself, and as a result, it will behave in accordance with this understanding.

Your thoughts carry a lot of weight. They are the ones responsible for the feelings that you experience. When you were sitting somewhere, did you ever notice that you were frustrated or furious about anything that happened earlier? You might not be sure why you are feeling so angry right now, but you are aware of the fact that you are, and as a result, you need to take a step back and examine the situation in greater depth. What is it that is causing you to feel that way and why do you feel that way? When you give it some thought, you come to the conclusion that, in the end, it is frequently the result of something that is completely unrelated to everything else that you are doing. It is essential that you keep this in mind: quite often, the issue was a completely unrelated notion that has been bothering you the whole time and causing so many problems for you. If you keep this in mind, you can begin to get a glimpse of what goes on inside the head of another person and how they process information.

Your feelings serve a very significant purpose; they keep you motivated to respond to the situation that you are in. This is an extremely important job that your feelings play. Every feeling you experience will have a function that is directly tied to your ability to stay alive throughout time. They all collaborate in order to create those acts that come naturally to you when you give in to the control that your emotions have over you. It is vital to keep this in mind because it means that if you feel yourself becoming emotionally invested in a particular action and then inspired to take that action, there is probably a reason for it. The range of feelings that you experience can be summed up in just seven categories:

Joy: You infuse yourself with joy so that you can encourage yourself to engage in that activity once more. It is something that was rewarding for whatever reason, and you have an innate desire to continue doing it since it was so beneficial.

When you have done something that has resulted in the loss of something important to you, you may experience feelings of sadness. Typically, this refers to an unfortunate event in which someone was harmed or lost. You experience feelings of regret as a result of being reminded that carrying out that behavior once more might be bad for a variety of reasons. It encourages you to look to other people for solace and assistance.

Angry: Being angry propels you to take action and fight back. In most cases, it is the result of feeling threatened for one reason or another and is intended to cause you to protect yourself or people around you in some way.

Fear: Fear is the emotion that drives you to take action to defend yourself from a danger that you are unable to overcome. When you are experiencing terror, you have the overwhelming want to flee the situation at any cost. If there is a means that you could potentially fight your way out of the predicament, fear can easily turn into anger. It will almost always result in you lashing out or trying to find a way to get out of the predicament you're in.

The state of being surprised is the result of your body's reaction to the fact that it needs to pay more attention to whatever is happening in your immediate environment. It forces you to concentrate on whatever is in front of you so that you may respond appropriately to the circumstance.

Contempt: Contempt is a sensation that is supposed to urge you to avoid someone else by making you feel inferior to them. It is essentially a combination of disgust and rage that is aimed toward a single individual.

Repulse: Repulse is intended to motivate you to steer clear of something that is detrimental to your health. When you come into contact with something that is putrid, whether in the literal or figurative sense, you get feelings of revulsion. Its purpose is to keep you separate from the issue and prevent you from becoming entangled in it in any manner. You persuade yourself that you have no choice but to steer clear of whatever it is that makes you feel repulsed.

As you can see, the feelings you experience serve a very vital function, and it is your responsibility to get an understanding of them. If you do not make an effort to actively counterbalance these feelings, they will become highly motivating and cause you to act in certain ways. It is true that you have the power to modify your behaviors on your own, but doing so is not always as simple as it sounds. It's possible to get caught in a bind if you don't know what you're doing. Your feelings have the potential to exert a strong influence over you. On the other hand, this indicates that you can generally look at what other people are doing in order to comprehend them as well. If you wanted to understand what was going on in the mind of another person, you would look at their behaviors since behaviors will follow whatever is happening in the mind of the person.

Consider it in this way: if you see someone racing at you with a frown and overall highly threatening body language, you can guess that they are upset about something. If they are running toward you with a frown and overall very threatening body language, you can conclude that they are angry with you. Once you have an understanding that they are extremely angry, you will be able to look at the situation and determine what the issue is. Have you just passed him in the parking lot without giving him enough space? It's possible that the fact that you took a seat will irritate him. Did you manage to hurt his feelings in some way? If that's the case, sort it out.

You may help yourself figure out what to do next by being able to follow these patterns in this manner and by having the ability to do so. It is possible to understand the attitudes that people are taking through all that they do simply by looking at them.

ACTIVITIES RELATED TO THERAPY

First, let's S.T.O.P.

Instead of giving in to a craving, try employing the S.T.O.P. approach, which stands for "think about where the craving is coming from." This is the S.T.O.P. approach, which stands for "stop, take a deep breath, look around, and then proceed." This strategy was developed by Elisha Goldstein, a psychologist, to aid individuals in returning their focus to the here and now. When one takes some time to organize one's thoughts before making a decision, that person is more likely to arrive at an informed choice.

Voici les directives: The next time you're faced with the want to give in to a need, here's what you should do:

1. Stop. Put an end to whatever it is that you're doing at the moment.

2. Inhale deeply; this will help you focus on the here and now by bringing your attention to the present moment.

3. Pay attention. Take a moment to take in your surroundings; you never know

when something exciting might take place outside. Think on how you are currently experiencing your emotions. Take detailed notes on the thoughts and feelings that are occurring within you. To put it another way, you need to pause for a moment and ask yourself, "What am I thinking?" How am I going to find out what I need to do in order to satiate this craving? What if I give in to this temptation and let myself go?

4. Continue on. Continue with whatever it was that you were doing before.

If you can train yourself to be present in the moment when a craving hits, it can help lessen the likelihood that you will participate in behavior that is harmful to you. Please include an explanation or justification for your response:

When you employed the S.T.O.P. technique, what did you discover about your desire to give in to it?

Avoid Giving In to the Urge Right Away

It is common to experience feelings of helplessness and being overwhelmed when one is in the midst of a need. Because you are putting so much emphasis on appeasing them, it gives them the impression that they are even more powerful. Even if just for a short period of time, you should make an effort to fight off the impulse to cave in.

After you've proven to yourself that you can resist the need to give in to a hunger for a short period of time, you'll have more confidence in your capacity to do so in the future. You can use the knowledge that you were able to resist the temptation the next time an unexpected temptation presents itself by remembering that you were successful in doing so. Your brain will learn to reject powerful desires if you train it in this way. The most effective approach for overcoming impulses is to have the ability to wait them out.

Voici les directives: If you feel a craving coming on, there are a few things you may do to delay its onset, including the following:

1. Become still and take a few long, slow breaths.

2. While looking around the room, select five unique things and then explain them out loud.

3. While it's important to take in your surroundings, you should also focus on how your body is feeling. After that, it's time to relax and give your muscles a chance to cool down.

4. While you count to 10, give some thought to your current physical experience. It's possible that as time goes on, you'll start to feel less of a desire to give in to your cravings for indulgence.

5. After five minutes, check in with yourself. Give yourself a pat on the back if you see that the requirement is becoming less pressing or has altogether vanished. If you need to, try again.

After you have finished the exercise, please respond to the questions that are listed below.

What was it that you required to quell the hunger in your stomach?

Putting an end to unproductive ideas or beliefs

In order to break some of our long-standing patterns, we need to take a closer look at what we believe. Negative thinking and the ways in which it influences our day-to-day decision-making need to be examined in order for us to effectively manage the things that need to be altered.

Only at that point will those who have been victimized be able to find glory by letting go of destructive beliefs and making place for more constructive ones. At that moment, we may now start training the brain to adapt to the new, more favorable environment that has been created.

It is of the utmost importance to deal with the problem of negative automatic thoughts (NATs). Before we move on, let's take a look at some of the ideas and other mental processes that occur in our minds.

A General Synopsis Of Our Opinions

Who are They, Exactly?
They are the thoughts that run through our heads. They consist of the things that we believe in, the standards that we desire to live by, our ethics and morals, what we perceive ourselves to be, and what the outside world teaches us.

Internal dialog
Even if we aren't always conscious of it, we are constantly storing and making meaning from the events that occur in our lives. People have a habit of constantly thinking about the things that surround them or have an effect on them, as if there is another person inside who is talking to them. Those who are knowledgeable in the field of psychology will refer to the internal dialogue that we have as 'self-talk.' It takes place not only in each of us but also within our brains, which is why it merits its own name. The conscious thoughts as well as

the subconscious ones are both a part of self-talk.

Feelings are influenced by our thoughts. What we believe and how we think about the world has a huge impact on how we make sense of the events that occur in our life. This includes both our attitudes and our beliefs. In a nutshell, our ideas are an accurate representation of our moods. There is a lot of enjoyment to be had in the future if an individual is able to learn how to maintain a happy attitude based on the linked motivations that nature supplies. If we allow ourselves to entertain negative thoughts, the opposite will also come to pass.

Our Thoughts Are Hard to Tame and Hardly Ever Under Our Control

Whether you choose to ignore the negative idea or not, you may rest assured that it, like the positive ones, will pass. Thoughts are nothing more than your interpretations of what you see and hear in the outer world, and as long as you remain conscious and alive, they will continue to come and go.

Not Everything That We Believe to Be True Is Actually the Case.

We get knowledge not only from our surroundings but also from how we interpret what we see. In light of this, there is a reason why we should not put one hundred percent of our faith in what we think. There are personal biases that are attached to the experiences that we have in life, and these will also influence the way that we think and understand things. In the end, we link what we have resulted in to meanings of the present, future or previous events; nevertheless, this does not necessarily guarantee that what we know is accurate.

a Fallacy in One's Thinking

Sometimes we think about the incorrect thing, and it could be something that we've been thinking about for a long time or something that comes up every once in a while. These kinds of thinking will keep you from conducting the appropriate examination of what you are going through, which will ultimately lead to the wrong conclusion being made. When this happens, you may find that you are thinking impulsively and making snap judgments, or even worse, that you are imagining the worst possible outcomes for a situation when you should be thinking sensibly. Cognitive distortions are another name for these types of erroneous ways of thinking because they come with warped ideas on how to approach different situations.

The thinking process is automatic.

As a component of automatic views, the negative automatic thoughts then make their appearance here. They always appear in our thoughts without our knowledge, and there is no indication that they are about to do so either. They are incorrect methods of thinking that offer detrimental ways of thinking about and interpreting what has happened in the world. Because of this, they should be avoided. The majority of us who are affected by these things are not going to be able to predict when they will strike, and we might not even be aware that they are harmful. If they happen frequently enough, the person will become accustomed to them to the point that they will stop questioning whether or not they are beneficial or acceptable in the first place.

The following is an illustration of NATs:

"No one likes me," the person said.

"No matter what I do, things are never going to work out."

"If I'm late, I won't be able to take advantage of this chance."

"I don't think it's true that I'm intelligent."

5. On the other hand, become skilled at responding with "Yes!" Occasionally Also

Did you know that being alone can be one of the most significant contributors to feelings of tension and anxiety? And it's not just people getting on in years who are affected; there's a growing number of young, successful individuals who, like you and I, are struggling in private with these tormenting feelings. In spite of the fact that these individuals could give off the impression that they are doing well, beneath the surface, they are actually suffering a great deal.

As a result, at the conclusion of a particularly trying day, they have developed the pattern of drawing the blinds, retreating into their den, and locking the door to enclose themselves and shield themselves from the cacophony of the outside world. They politely decline all of those great social invites and end up missing out on so much just because they allow their anxiety and worry to dictate their decisions.

The paradox is that at this point in their lives, they require human interaction more than anything else. They require the presence of someone who will provide them with constant support and reassure them that everything will be okay.

It's possible that they feel this way because, at some point in the past, they "burned out." Perhaps there are certain things in their past that they wish they could change. Perhaps they are struggling under the weight of a crippling case of social anxiety. Alternately, it's possible that they just aren't the outgoing type. Does any of this ring true for you?

If that's the case, I strongly encourage you to begin responding "yes." By venturing outside of your comfort zone, you might be pleasantly surprised to discover how much better you feel as a direct result.

6. Make the Most of Your "Down Time"

Sitting still and doing nothing at all is not always the easiest thing to do, despite the fact that it seems like it should be the simplest thing in the world. It is extremely crucial that you do find time to disconnect from the craziness of the world, especially if you value your mental health. If you respect your mental health, you should find time to withdraw from the confusion of the world.

The real world is rife with diversions. The barrage of information that comes at us from every direction in this day and age is extremely difficult, if not impossible, to avoid. This, in turn, traps you, overwhelms your senses with so-called "noise," and makes you feel a great deal worse rather than a great deal better.

Make turning off your device a top priority at regular intervals. Turn off all of your electronic devices and give yourself some downtime. Try going for a slow stroll in the open air, picking up a book that will improve your spirits, or catching up with a good friend instead.

7. Make a habit out of being mindful.

There are times when we allow ourselves to become so preoccupied with our own thoughts that we forget to be present in the world around us. As a result, we miss out on a significant portion of the splendor that is life. Instead than focusing on the joy that surrounds us, our attention is drawn to the looming deadlines and onerous tasks. Therefore, make an effort to slow down, open your eyes to the things that are immediately surrounding you, and search for reasons to be appreciative and grateful.

8. Try some deep meditation.

No longer solely practiced by members of the "green" community, meditation is rapidly becoming one of the most widely practiced methods for self-improvement and overall health and wellness. Your heart rate can be lowered, the balance of your hormones can be restored, you can become more aware, and your response to stress can be halted dead in its tracks if you practice on a regular basis. Why not give it a shot? Set a goal for yourself to meditate every day for the next month and see how much better you feel at the end of it. Here is a fantastic activity with which you can get started.

The Practice of Meditation:

Place yourself in a relaxed position where you won't be disturbed for the duration of your practice, and then set the timer on your watch or other device for the specified amount of time. Even just ten minutes can be very productive, particularly when you first get started.

Take up a relaxed posture with your feet planted firmly on the ground and your hands softly propped up in the crooks of your knees.

Now, direct your attention to the flow of your breath as it enters and exits your body. Pay attention to this process. Do not make any attempts to alter it; rather, just observe it.

You should start counting your inhalations at one and work your way up to ten, after which you should repeat the process for as long as you see fit.

Then, begin counting your exhalations from one all the way up to ten once more, and continue doing so until you get the urge to switch to a different method.

While you are concentrating your attention in this way, make an effort to let as much of your mental tension go as you can. It is not necessary for you to concentrate on emptying your mind; rather, you should simply acknowledge your ideas and let them pass you by while you sit quietly. You might find that doing this is challenging at first, but as long as you keep practicing, your skills will continue to grow.

After the prescribed amount of time has passed, you can simply open your eyes and ease back into the real world.

You should be congratulated; you have just mastered the art of meditation.

Feelings Of Happiness And A Healthy Body Go Hand In Hand.

Not only may a person who is experiencing happy emotions aid that person to improve their cerebral abilities, but positive emotions can also help that person improve their physical health. It should come as no surprise that eating well and staying active are two essential components of leading a healthy lifestyle. In spite of this, there have been studies done in recent years that have established a connection between getting a regular dose of any happy emotion and having better physical health.

In a recent study, researchers went one step further in investigating the link between healthy physical states and happy mental states. Not only does the research demonstrate that people's health can be improved by having happy emotions, but it is also able to determine how positive emotions are able to have this effect in the first place. The findings of the study led the researchers to the conclusion that persons who experience good emotions have the possibility to feel more socially linked to other people. In the research study, there were a total of 65 participants split into two distinct groups. One group was instructed in a practice known as loving-kindness meditation, while the other group was placed on a waiting list to participate in the medication training. Both groups were given the opportunity to learn about both practices. There was not a single participant who had any prior experience with the practice of meditation, despite the fact that all of them worked as professors at the University of North Carolina.

The practice of loving-kindness meditation was selected because its goal is to educate participants on how to create intensified feelings of love, compassion, and general goodness toward oneself as well as towards other individuals.

In addition to taking part in the meditation group, the participants also participated in a class that met once a week for one hour and lasted for a total of six weeks. During the period of the sessions, the participants were also requested to use some everyday practices while they were at home in addition to participating in the lessons themselves.

Participants in both groups were requested to maintain a record on a daily basis throughout the entirety of the training session, in addition to the two weeks leading up to the training and the week following its conclusion. The reports were intended to keep track of the amount of time that they were spending meditating, the emotions that they were feeling the strongest on a particular day, and the quality of each of their social contacts with other people.

The health of the participants was evaluated both before the training began and after it was finished by the researchers. This was done both before and after the training was given. In order to accomplish this, the researchers monitored their subjects' heart rates as well as their breathing patterns and recorded readings of both. The manner in which one could determine the "tone" of a person's vagus nerve was the primary topic of discussion. Because it serves as a connection between the brain and the body, this nerve is responsible for regulating an individual's heart rate.

Because of its link to people's cardiovascular health, researchers found vagal tone to be such an appropriate objective indicator for the participants' overall physical wellness. This is due to the fact that vagal tone has a connection to cardiovascular health.

Over the course of their training, those who participated in loving-kindness meditation showed a more substantial increase in pleasant feelings such as amazement, appreciation, and amusement than those who were on the waiting list to meditate. This was the case when compared to those on the waiting list to meditate.

Those people who demonstrated a more significant increase in their pleasant emotions over the course of the study were also much more likely to report feeling socially connected to other people as the study progressed. These individuals reported that as a result, they felt closer to and more "in tune" with the other people in their immediate environment. This indicates that the improvements in people's vagal tone are linked to the fact that they experience a stronger social connection to other people.

The findings of the study ultimately presented some of the most compelling evidence to date that experiencing good emotions might, in fact, have a beneficial effect on a person's physical health. The results of the study were also able to demonstrate that directly feeling pleasant emotions is not sufficient on its own to improve a person's physical and mental health to a sufficient degree. The strength of a person's pleasant feelings in relation to the strength of the connections they have with other people is instead the primary consideration in this equation.

It turned out that this particular investigation was the very first one of its kind to ever illustrate how social connectivity serves as the essential link that connects having pleasant emotions with having improved health. All of the findings are incredibly significant due to the fact that they imply that people can enhance their own health by taking the steps that are the most basic and practicable. Because of this, the findings of the study should serve as motivation for individuals to place a higher priority on the frequency with which they connect with other people, even if this just entails doing actions such as picking up the phone or sending a text message to a friend.

If a person is unable to connect with other people at a specific time, it is likely that they will be able to do so in the future if they work on honing their more positive feelings in their own time and according to their own standards.

That signifies that as people experience more positive emotions throughout their life - whether it be through the utilization of the loving-kindness meditation, focusing one's thoughts on positive memories, or indulging in activities that a person enjoys - they are most likely taking care of their bodies in addition to their minds. This is because positive emotions have been shown to have a positive impact on a person's likelihood of living a longer, healthier life.

The central finding that emerged from a large number of investigations and discussions on the topic of pleasant emotions was the concept that these feelings function as a "upward spiral" because they are associated with improved physical health for individuals. The loop of having pleasant emotions and being in good health then continues since studies has shown that being in excellent health also results in more of those great feelings being generated.

According to the findings of some studies, repeating experiences of happy emotions can act as a source of nutrients for the body. This is due to the fact that positive feelings have been shown to result in an increased sense of social belonging in a person. People who experience pleasant emotions also receive the required boost they need to activate their parasympathetic health, which then leads to the opening up to the possibility of experiencing even more positive emotions as well as social encounters that are fulfilling.

How To Conquer Anxiety And Live Your Life To The Fullest

In an ideal world, you would never experience the kinds of feelings and ideas that can bring on an anxiety attack or a panic attack. However, given that you are a human being, it is inevitable that you will worry about many things. However, if you find that you are beginning to panic, there are a number of simple actions that you can take to settle your mind, redirect your thoughts, relax your body, brighten your day, and get back into the action-packed game that is commonly known as life.

You have the power to determine how difficult or enjoyable your life will be. If worry is the primary factor preventing you from experiencing joy in life, give the following tried-and-true strategies a shot:

1. Quit being so hard on yourself.

Learn to have a positive relationship with yourself first. When you have an anxiety condition, you are more inclined to blame yourself for unpleasant panic attacks like the ones you've been having. Be gentle with yourself and treat yourself with the same compassion, support, and kindness that you would show to someone else who was suffering from a certain sickness. Compassion is a powerful antidote that, when practiced, has the ability to heal both fresh and old wounds, as well as foster a sense of inner peace and contentment in its recipients.

You are not to fault for your concern; therefore, you should refrain from placing blame on yourself and from working against yourself. Playing the blame game can lead to self-destruction and a deep melancholy, whereas practicing compassion can help you turn panic into tranquility and maintain your happiness over the long term.

2. Get ready for the day that lies ahead.

Create productive routines for yourself to fight the nervous thoughts that keep popping into your head. Create a to-do list or a plan so that your attention is kept focused on the necessary activities, rather than worrisome thoughts, rather than spending twenty minutes of every morning worrying about the day or frantically searching for your phone or keys. This will save you time.

3. Give yourself permission to worry every day

Are you out of your mind? What kind of advice are you giving? It's possible that I've lost my mind, but I think that worrying is perfectly OK; the catch is that it can only be done so for a limited period of time. Because my day is so jam-packed and I can sense when I'm ready to have a panic attack, I make sure to leave myself a cushion of 15 minutes each day to focus on my anxiety. After 15 minutes have passed, I tell myself, "So, you had enough time to worry, and now let's tackle the next task on the list." At that point, I stop thinking about it and tell myself, "So, you had enough time to worry, and now let's tackle the next task on the list."

4. Step away from your device every once in a while.

Plan a period of time during which you will be able to entirely unplug, even if it's just for ten minutes. That means no checking emails or the phone, turning off the television or news, and doing absolutely nothing else. Your level of stress and the risk of having a panic attack will both decrease as a result of this. You'll find that you're much happier with your lifestyle if you make it a point to disconnect from technology on a daily basis and, if at all possible, do so twice a day.

5. Make a cheerful vision board for yourself.

Changing the way you think about what's in store for you in the future can help if the future appears unpredictable and frightening to you. Making a vision board might help you create a happy future for yourself. The simple process of choosing objectives that are both enjoyable and attainable might alleviate some of the stress associated with worrying about the unknown future.

Spend at least an hour and a half crafting a positive vision board depicting the things you hope to achieve in the not-too-distant future. Make sure that you create a board that is as realistic as possible to protect yourself from being let down and experiencing more severe anxiety. If you aren't the crafty kind, you might want to think about creating a happy electronic vision board with the assistance of Pinterest. When you are doing it, make sure you stick to the T.H.I.N.K. technique: Are the things I'm thinking about Genuine, Beneficial, Inspiring, Essential, and Kind?

6. Educate yourself on how to breathe properly throughout the day.

Learning how to breathe properly throughout the day is one of the most essential skills for preventing anxiety and living life to the fullest possible extent. Breathing that is shallow and rapid is a physical manifestation of anxiety and stress in the body and brain. On the other hand, purposefully deep breathing, combined with strengthening and stretching the breath, helps to convey messages to your brain that it's okay to feel relaxed. This is especially helpful if you're experiencing anxiety or stress.

7. Give your body the fuel it needs by eating properly.

Anxiety disorders have the potential to throw your body off-kilter. Your appetite can shift, and you may start to crave foods you never used to be interested in eating. However, in order to give your body the assistance it need, you should reevaluate the foods you eat on a regular basis and choose to consume more foods that are rich in nutrients such as omega-3 fatty acids and vitamin B.

In addition to that, make sure that the carbohydrates you consume on a regular basis come from whole grains. Vitamin B has also been linked to improved mental health, as have omega-3 fatty acids, which have been shown in a number of studies to lessen the symptoms of anxiety and sadness. Carbohydrates from whole grains contribute to the maintenance of healthy levels of serotonin, the "feel-good" neurotransmitter that is responsible for promoting feelings of contentment and serenity.

Because eating processed foods and sugar might make anxiety symptoms worse, you should try to reduce how much of both you eat.

8. Make it a routine to keep a smile on your face throughout the day.

Are you experiencing feelings of anxiety? Cheer up! Are you having an attack of panic right now? Have some fun. When dealing with anxiety symptoms, it might be helpful to "fake" a smile or chuckle in order to make it through the day. Have you ever witnessed someone smiling or laughing despite being in a potentially harmful situation? It is not an indication that one has gone insane; rather, it is merely a joyful approach to deal with the negativity that is all around us. If you give it some practice, you'll be able to understand what I mean by it.

9. Be sure to get enough sleep.

A lack of quality sleep can have major negative effects, including negative effects on your physical health and a contribution to the total tension and worry you feel. Additionally, because anxiety disorders sometimes contribute to insomnia, not getting enough quality sleep can sometimes become a self-perpetuating cycle. When you are feeling anxious, try scheduling a full 7 to 9 hours of sleep time, taking short naps throughout the day, and observing what the effects of sound sleep have on your levels of anxiety.

10. Devote more of your time to the people who are both important to you and who adore you.

People who love you can make it easier for you to recover from traumatic experiences like divorce, unemployment, and the loss of a job. These people can be friends or family members. Make sure that no matter how busy you are, you always have enough time to hang out with your closest friends, have meaningful conversations with your parents, and have fun with your children.

11. Physical activity

People who suffer from anxiety and panic attacks often find that working exercise helps them feel better. Endorphins and other chemicals in the brain that are related with reducing anxiety and sadness can be triggered by engaging in regular physical activity. Additionally, it raises the temperature of your body, which helps you relax and boosts your immune system, lowering the likelihood that you may experience depression as a result. People who suffer from anxiety problems can benefit enormously by taking up running.

Developing Your Own Self-Assurance While Engaging In Conversation

Nobody is born with an unshakeable sense of self-worth and confidence. If someone gives off the impression of having an extraordinary amount of self-assurance, it is likely that they have spent a significant amount of time and effort cultivating that trait. Because the demanding world of business and life in general have a tendency to deflate one's self-confidence, it is something that must be learned to be able to be built up.

Our self-confidence can suffer when we receive unfavorable feedback in the form of a poor online review, a request for a refund from a consumer, or an outright rejection from potential investors. Comments from people closest to us, even if they are well intentioned yet occasionally cruel, can also cut us deeply.

On top of all of this, we have to contend with the self-doubt and inner critic that are constantly telling us that we are not adequate in some way. When we are confronted by a barrage of factors that pose a threat to our self-confidence, it is imperative that we take responsibility for bolstering it on our own.

People that exude confidence are seen as more attractive, they are more successful in sales, and they are able to perform admirably in front of an audience. They are also confident in their ability to deal with any challenges life may bring them and are willing to take greater risks, which naturally results in opening up opportunities.

It's not true that everyone is born with an innate feeling of confidence in themselves. If you struggle with low self-esteem or have had personal situations that have caused you to lose confidence, it can be difficult to develop confidence at times. This could be because of one of these factors.

A confident person is someone who: does what they believe is right, even if it's controversial; is prepared to take risks; admits their mistakes; learns from their mistakes; is optimistic; can accept compliments; and does all of the following.

There are a number of different things you can perform to bolster your self-assurance. There are some of them that require only slight adjustments to how you think, while others will require more time and effort on your part before they become second nature.

Consider all that you have already accomplished.

If you believe that you haven't accomplished anything, it's easy to lose confidence in yourself. Create a list of all the accomplishments you've had in your life that you're pleased with, such as receiving a good grade on a test or becoming proficient at surfing. Maintain a close proximity to the list, and add to it anytime you accomplish anything that fills you with satisfaction. When you're feeling insecure about yourself, take out the list and use it to remind yourself of all the amazing things you've accomplished in the past.

Consider the things that you excel at because everyone has different skills and capabilities. Which ones do you have? Confidence in one's skills can be increased by first recognizing one's strengths and then working to improve upon those strengths. Trying to improve upon one's strengths will allow one to feel more capable.

Establish some aims for yourself.

Create some objectives for yourself, and then map out the actions that will get you there. Baking a cake or organizing a get-together with friends can also count as accomplishing little goals, so don't feel pressured to set lofty ambitions for yourself. Simply set your sights on a few manageable goals that you will be able to cross off a list once you have accomplished them. This will make you feel more confident in your abilities to get things done.

Be positive about yourself.

If you constantly berate yourself in your head and convince yourself that you're not good enough, you'll never be able to feel confidence in yourself. Consider how the way you talk to yourself could be influencing your self-confidence and how you could change it. Be as kind to yourself as you would be to your closest friend, and encourage yourself wherever you can.

Take up a pastime.

Make an effort to become interested in something outside of work. It could be anything from photography to sports to knitting, or even something completely different! When you've identified what drives you, make a pact with yourself to give that pursuit a shot. If you have a strong interest in or enthusiasm for a certain activity, you will almost certainly be more driven to participate in that activity, and you will also develop your talents more rapidly.

Always be prepared to share an interesting tale with others.

Even if your life is very uneventful and devoid of excitement or intrigue most of the time, you should still be able to provide a response to the inquiry "What's new?" that is more interesting than "Not much." People who are self-assured tend to be effective conversationalists, although this is a talent that requires more effort for certain people than for others. Are you making preparations for a trip? Are you renovating a portion of your home? Taking your children to a variety of sporting events? Have a significant amount of time and effort invested in a significant project at work that requires your attention? When someone starts a discussion with you, think of something intriguing to say to continue the exchange.

Maintain an upright stance.

Slouching sends the message that you do not have faith in yourself and should be avoided. If you find that this is an area in which you struggle, you could find it helpful to write a reminder on the outside border of your computer screen using a thick red marker, such as an up arrow. Roll your shoulders back and envision drawing a rope from the top of your head, which will elongate your spine and raise your chin so that it is in a neutral, forward-facing position. This will rectify the posture that you are currently exhibiting.

Put an end to your concern over what other people will think.

People who struggle with their confidence often find that they are unable to be present and be the greatest version of themselves if they are constantly questioning themselves about whether or not they come off as confident. Did they consider me to be a clever person? Did they have the impression that I had achieved success? Did they think I was being foolish when I said that? In point of fact, it is impossible to ever truly know what the thoughts of another person are regarding you.

Therefore, rather than worrying about it, focus on what you want to say, such as asking the appropriate questions, avoiding time-wasting small talk, and making eye contact with the other person.

Put an end to your critical internal monologue.

Take note of the things that you keep repeating to yourself in your head and pay attention to them. Replace negative thoughts like "I can't do this" with more constructive ones like "I'm going to give it my best shot" if you find yourself thinking something negative. The trick is to take a step back from yourself and examine your internal monologue as an objective observer might. How would you react if the person sitting next to you said anything along the lines of, "I'm so [fat, dumb, ugly, slow, etc.]?" That's quite severe, isn't it? Take the time to care for yourself and your thought life the same way you would for another person.

Spend money on improving your appearance.

People who take care of themselves on the outside, whether by getting a new haircut, buying new clothes, taking care of dental issues, or seeing an esthetician, report having a greater sense of well-being on the inside. No matter how attractive a person actually is or what their social standing is, those who believe they are more physically attractive have a higher perception of the social class to which they belong. This is true regardless of how gorgeous a person actually is.

Gratitude And Acknowledgment

It is essential that you are able to demonstrate gratitude, humility, and a sense of grace toward the interviewer and the HR team when you are given the opportunity to participate in an interview. If you are given this opportunity, you should know how to say "thank you." There is a good chance that HR has considered applications from a wide variety of individuals. They have invested a significant amount of time in reviewing the applications, and as a result, they have performed a significant amount of labor in order to select candidates who are qualified to perform the duties of the position. They chose you for a specific reason; yet, it is obvious that it was a time-consuming process for them to sort through all of the applications before arriving at yours. Because of this, you ought to be grateful that the interview was even granted to you in the first place.

When you enter into the room, you should say "thank you" right away, and you should continue to say it throughout the interview. This will show that you are thankful. This is a stage that many people skip and do not remember, but by completing it, you exhibit a level of competency that is higher than the average candidate would have. You ought to respond to the interviewer with anything along these lines, therefore: I am grateful that you asked me to participate in this interview. I want to express my gratitude for taking the time out of your busy schedule to speak with me about this open position. It is not necessary for you to embellish your language or make an effort to make it sound more sophisticated. Instead, make it straightforward and to the point so that you can express your appreciation to the person who is interviewing you.

You should express gratitude to the person conducting the interview not only at the beginning of the interview, but also at the conclusion of the interview as well. Even if you don't get the job or the interview doesn't go well, you can still thank the interviewer for his or her time because they will likely be seeing a lot of candidates and have to make decisions based on the interview results. It is crucial to begin and end with appreciation because even if you don't get the job or the interview doesn't go well, you can still thank the interviewer for his or her time. Taking time out of their packed schedule to participate in these interviews can prove to be a nuisance for them. It is a costly endeavor to either replace an employee or hire a new one, so you need to make sure that you give careful consideration to the amount of time, money, and investment that you put into these interviews. It is not something that is something that is simple for a place of business to perform. At the end of the interview, you need to make a closing statement along the lines of "Thank you once more for your time and consideration." I wanted to express my gratitude for the opportunity to discuss this position with you. I hope you enjoy your day.

The Note of Appreciation

Another action that goes beyond the call of duty is writing a note of gratitude to the recipient of the favor. If you are willing to do something that the vast majority of other candidates won't, then you will set yourself apart from the competition and become an exceptional candidate. At the end of the interview, many people fail to express their gratitude for the opportunity. In most cases, it does not certain that you will receive an offer of employment. Do not fall into the trap of assuming that writing a thank-you card would automatically result in you being offered the position; nonetheless, it is something that can assist remind the interviewer of both you and your experience interviewing them. When they are considering a number of candidates and need to differentiate between them in the results, this is of the utmost importance. You will be able to differentiate yourself from the other candidates and demonstrate that you are serious and truly interested in getting the job if you send a thank you note following an interview. Share your thoughts and feelings through writing, and elaborate on your experience with the interview. The following are some suggestions for drafting a note of gratitude to a recipient.

Start by being grateful.

The very first thing that you should say is something along the lines of "I want to express my gratitude for taking the time to talk to me about this opportunity." I am grateful that I was given the opportunity to learn more about the position and how I could contribute to this firm.

You should convey to the interviewer how much you valued the time they spent with you and then discuss the nature of your experience in the interview.

Discuss the ways in which the organization supports you in achieving your objectives.

Next, you need to explain how the core values of the organization connect with the directions you want to take your career in the future. Discuss the applicable experience and talents you possess, as well as how you believe they would assist you succeed in this role. Mention the types of job obligations that you would be expected to carry out and talk about how your experience will assist you complete everything that you need to do in order to succeed in this position. Discuss the ways in which the core values of the organization coincide with the professional goals you have set for yourself. This will help demonstrate to the firm that you are a suitable fit for the role that they have available.

Mention something that you weren't able to go into detail about during the interview.

You should also highlight something that you were unable to say during the interview, either because there was not enough time allotted for the question and answer session or because you forgot to include it in your responses. This will demonstrate to the interviewer that you were able to remember something significant and that you wished to bring it to their attention. After that, the person conducting the interview will also be aware that you are a good candidate for the job.

Discuss the reasons why you are the most qualified applicant.

In conclusion, you need to make a powerful impression on the hiring manager by demonstrating why you are the best possible candidate for this position. In this section, you need to restate your talents and experience and discuss how those things make you the most qualified candidate for this position. Do not be bashful about discussing your professional accomplishments, and be sure to emphasize the aspects of your background that are most relevant to demonstrating why you would be a great choice for this position.

Putting Yourself Out There And Seeking Assistance Along With Surrounding Yourself With Support

At first, the thought of conquering your depression may appear to be unattainable or more than you are able to bear. Try not to become overly anxious. Your hopelessness and helplessness are not reflective of the world around you; rather, they are only another sign of the mental illness that you suffer from. These emotions do not indicate that you are incapable of growing or that you lack strength in any way. Beginning with manageable goals and being open to receiving assistance are two essential components of successful recovery from depression. It might be really beneficial to simply discuss your emotions with another person in direct conversation. It is not necessary for this individual to be a trained professional or someone who can solve all of your issues; rather, they should simply be compassionate and attentive to your concerns.

Your road to rehabilitation will go much more quickly if you are surrounded by a strong network of support from people who care about you. They claim that being alone is one of the biggest contributors to depression. Because of this, you should make it a point to constantly reach out to the people around you, even if you prefer to be alone yourself or don't want to burden anyone else. To tell you the truth, the vast majority of individuals will be relieved to learn that you have chosen to confide in them about your problems. It is a great compliment to feel that someone trusts and relies on you. Therefore, you should make your friends and family aware of what is going on in your life and ask them what they can do to assist you in obtaining the necessary support.

Methods To Either Completely Eliminate Or Significantly Reduce Anxiety

Anxiety is something that few people look forward to, yet a lot of individuals can become skilled at managing it. The assumption that most individuals make is that the discomfort associated with anxiety is constantly present. The reality is that there are times when feeling anxious does not cause the same level of discomfort as other times. When you ride a roller coaster for the first time, you will most certainly feel some level of nervousness as the cars are being hauled up the first hill. It is completely understandable to feel anxious. The fact that most individuals are unable to fly contributes to their fear of heights. Because of this, the outcomes would be devastating in the event that anything unexpected occurred and they ended up falling. The vast majority of people are wary of novel and challenging situations because they are unsure of their ability to cope with them. We experience those sentiments despite the fact that we are aware of the fact that it is extremely unlikely that riding the roller coaster will put our lives in danger. In point of fact, if we believed that it could endanger our lives, going on the roller coaster would be an extremely foolish choice to make.

The fact that our feelings might shift throughout an event, such as riding a roller coaster, is an intriguing aspect of such activities. Many folks, once they've had a few turns on the roller coaster, find that they can't wait to go back for more. What is their level of interest in riding that roller coaster once more? Enough that they have to wait in line for a total of ninety minutes before they are allowed to try their luck. What exactly is going on here? It is obvious that the nervousness that is an inherent part of your first time riding a roller coaster has been in some way transferred to another experience that we might describe as thrilling. This is a smooth progression of events. It is not something that is exclusive to roller coasters. Skydivers consistently describe the occurrence of the same phenomenon. People who give physically demanding performances in front of large audiences have reported experiencing the same phenomenon. At first, a person is going to feel a great deal of anxiety, but through repeated exposure, they will learn how to control their worry. However, the evidence demonstrates something that is quite fascinating. The individual continues to experience the physiological responses that are often linked with anxiety. The time course of these physiological responses, however, shifts. For inexperienced skydivers, the moment they step out of the airplane is the moment when they feel the most dread. When I talk about peak anxiety, what I'm really referring about is the physiological responsiveness that comes with the anxiety reaction. Skydivers with years of experience reach almost the same peak of physiological arousal, but they reach that peak right before they step out of the plane. According to

Epstein and Fenz (1965), when people leave an environment, their physiological sensitivity typically declines. In the following section, I will discuss the possible causes of this long-standing phenomena.

In this chapter, the majority of our attention is concentrated on the different ways that one can deal with worry. The vast majority of people understand "managing anxiety" to imply "minimizing anxiety," and our attention is focused on how to accomplish this objective. However, there are some circumstances in which reducing worry to the lowest possible level is not an appropriate goal. We will discuss these scenarios, how to recognize them, and what to do when you find yourself in one of these predicaments. The most important thing to remember for the time being is that anxiety can be managed, and that with enough work, you can learn to manage your own worry.

As a Form of Behavioral Indicator, Anxiety

Anxiety has been discussed as a behavioral indicator indicating there may be a risk in the future, and it has been suggested that it would be prudent to take this into consideration while making future plans. Although it would be very challenging to show, this behavioral signal is most likely a holdover from our evolutionary past. However, doing so would not be impossible. There are a lot of behavioral cues that we share with other animals, and the behaviors that are driven by these signals are quite important. The fact that we share them with other animals and that they are important to survival argues for an evolutionary origin, but from the standpoint of this book, the origin of anxiety is unimportant. Because we share them with other animals and because they are important to survival.

Anxiety is significant because it is both a clear warning of suffering and an indicator that attention and even action may be wise at this time. Both of these things are relevant. In the prior chapter, we discussed the process of assessing the factors that bring on feelings of anxiety as well as the behavioral reactions one has when feeling worried. That evaluation ought to be the first thing that one does in reaction to any kind of anxious sensation. Exactly what are you concerned about right now? What kind of circumstance, thinking, or piece of information brought on your anxious feelings? What are the actual dangers that you are exposed to, in what kinds of circumstances will you be exposed to those risks, and at what times will those risks manifest themselves? What steps can you take to lower your exposure to those dangers? And ultimately, when weighed against the potential benefits of taking such risks, do you believe they are worth the potential downsides?

I really wish I could tell you that there is a straightforward response to each of those questions, but I just can't.

You may be able to provide answers that are acceptable in certain circumstances by drawing from your personal experience in the relevant circumstances as well as the information that you can obtain from other sources. Having said that, there are circumstances in which you have access to a restricted amount of information yet are nevertheless required to make a decision regarding what to do. In conclusion, a portion of your choice is determined by factors that are unique to you and are a product of the value system that you hold.

Consider the question, "How much of a risk are you willing to take?" as an illustration of a personal decision. What kind of return do you anticipate receiving in exchange for the amount of risk that you are taking? If you apply for a job and you get rejected, for instance, it will be a blow to your ego. This is only one of the dangers associated with applying for any job. However, there is a possibility that there are additional risks involved. For instance, it is not outside the realm of possibility that you may be employed by a company that would terminate your employment if they learned that you were actively seeking employment with another company. Therefore, doing interviews with other companies puts your existing career in jeopardy. Is there too much at stake there? The answer to this question is dependent on a number of factors, including the likelihood that the new employer will discover you, the probability that they will recruit you, and the quality of the potential new employment in comparison to your existing position. Unfortunately, in most situations, it is hard to determine the likelihood of each of these dangers; therefore, the most that can be done is to make educated guesses about how likely each risk is.

There are other scenarios in which the danger is readily apparent while the potential reward is less obvious; despite this, many individuals come to the conclusion that taking the risk is worthwhile. As an illustration, there are individuals who opt to participate in skydiving. Although it might not sound like your idea of a good time, some people find enjoyment in activities such as jumping out of perfectly decent airplanes. They are aware of the potential dangers, and it is clear that one of their primary goals is to minimize those dangers to the greatest extent feasible. They might decide to go skydiving despite the dangers involved since taking chances is how they like to have fun. They do not believe that participating in skydiving will improve their chances of being successful in their careers or that it will assist them in finding the person they will marry.

I am not trying to hide the fact that I formerly had a profession in skydiving. when of a sudden change in the wind direction on my second jump, the experience was cut short when I ended up in a cornfield. My leg was broken in four places, and I did significant damage to both the tendon and the ligament as I fell awkwardly and landed hard on my ankle. Before I got hurt, I had the ability to slam dunk a basketball. Following that injury, I was only able to hop three inches off the ground when I jumped. Despite this, I do not feel any remorse over my choice to go skydiving. It was a wonderful experience, and it provided me with the chance to show that I could perform a dangerous activity despite my personal nervousness and that I could do so successfully. Having said that, I have talked to many people who have gone skydiving and informed me that they were totally persuaded that if anything went wrong, they would not have been capable of doing what was required to survive. These people have told me that they went into the experience with the conviction that they would not be able to survive. I apologize, but in my opinion, that is completely insane. I did not share my thoughts with them, but it is what I was considering saying to them. I would never have jumped out of the plane if I did not feel confident in my ability to recognize a problem and take the necessary measures to save my life if it presented itself. My desire to die is not currently present, nor has it ever been there in my life.

Not only did I participate in a tandem skydiving when I was younger, but when I was older, I also learned how to pilot a plane on my own. This was done in part to highlight the peculiar nature of anxiety triggers. You might conclude that I do not have a fear of heights based on the fact that I have participated in each of those activities. But the truth is that I have a severe phobia of heights. I have a terrible fear of heights and would never want to be on a roof or a ladder that is higher than fifteen feet. When I was younger, I used to force myself to complete critical homeowner's activities since, to tell you the truth, I did not have the money to pay other people to do them. After that, I would get the house ready for painting, remove anything that was on the roof, and clean out the gutters. When I finally had the financial means to do so, I stopped doing those things myself and instead hired other people to do them for me. The first home that I ever owned was a multi-story structure with two and a half levels. When the roof needed to be replaced, I solicited many estimates, and one of the bids was submitted by an eighty-year-old gentleman who methodically walked around our roof to establish what was required. I chose his bid because he was the most reasonable. When he came down from the roof, I conveyed my astonishment at how comfortable he had become up there. He claimed that it was nothing more than a large hill, but I insisted that it was actually a hill with a cliff halfway down it. If someone could just remove the roof from the home and place it in the backyard, I would be more than delighted to take a stroll on it.

You might have experience with scenarios that are comparable to the ones you wish to avoid because they cause you to experience overwhelming anxiety. Perhaps you have examples of how you have handled situations that are anxiety-provoking in the past and continue to do so. Sometimes, there are valid reasons that can explain why your attitude to these identical events is different from what it would be in other similar scenarios. There are times when there are no readily apparent explanations that could explain the divergent response. I might make the case that, contrary to popular belief, the number one cause of accidental death in the United States is falling off of ladders and roofs. That offers an argument that, at first glance, appears to have some merit. If, on the other hand, you have a solid grasp of statistics, you will see that this reasoning is fallacious. There are significantly more fatalities associated with climbing on ladders than there are with skydiving because many more people participate in the activity of climbing on ladders, whereas very few people would ever consider participating in skydiving. Skydiving still poses a greater risk than mounting a ladder, despite the fact that both activities are potentially dangerous.

What helps you keep your body and mind at ease?

Questions Regarding the Identification of What the World Requires

You can also ask yourself questions concerning the ways in which you can assist other people, such as the following:

What are the most common questions that people have for you?

What do you think the rest of the world is lacking that you have in excess, and why do you believe this?

What sort of mark do you hope to make on the world with your life?

What kinds of things could you do to get involved in the life of your community?

What can you bring to the table for the benefit of others?

Questions Regarding the Process of Discovering Your Strong Suits

Answering these questions will assist you in locating some of your latent capabilities, which will lead you closer to locating your Ikigai:

What sorts of things do you like to do when you have some free time?

Which of your skills do you find you pick up quickly?

What are some of the accomplishments you've attained over the course of your life?

Which of your skills do people compliment you on the most often?

What does it mean to you to be successful?

Questions Regarding the Process of Discovering What You Are Capable of Being Paid For

Although the traditional definition of Ikigai does not explain purpose as being tied to financial gain, there are a few questions about your employment that you may ask yourself to help you uncover your Ikigai. These questions are as follows:

What kinds of things would you undertake with your time if financial concerns weren't an issue?

In what kind of an atmosphere at work do you think you could find happiness?

In a professional environment, which values are most important to you?

What are the things that people around the world or in your town value?

What benefits can you provide to other people?

The Application Of Thought Journals To Disorders Of Social Anxiety

We have previously discussed the concept of keeping a journal at several points throughout this book; nevertheless, I would like to go into additional detail about it because it can be such an important component of your recovery process. In the therapy of social anxiety disorder, thought recordings, which are also often referred to as thought diaries, are frequently employed. People can better comprehend their negative thought patterns through them, which paves the way for them to change those patterns. The model of cognitive-behavioral therapy is based on the premise that one's behaviors and emotions can be altered due to the fact that they are, at least in part, the outcome of one's own thoughts. The ABC behavior model was developed by the psychologist Albert Ellis, and it goes as follows:

A catalyst is something that sets off a chain reaction that leads to B being the thoughts and beliefs that lead to C being the outcomes of those thoughts and beliefs.

It could appear to a lot of individuals that the circumstances in their lives are directly responsible for the emotions they feel, but you might be surprised to find out that there is actually an additional stage in between the circumstance and the emotions it elicits. This step will manifest itself as your own internal ideas. When it comes to determining how you feel about a person or a circumstance, perception plays a significant role. However, for the majority of us, the thought process is so natural that we don't even recognize that we've had particular ideas.

Take a moment to recall the many different sorts of therapies that have already been discussed here and that concentrate on mental processes. The usage of a thought record can be of considerable use in a variety of practices, including hypnosis, mindful meditation, and guided imagery, amongst others.

Let's pretend for a second that you are at a party and you are chit-chatting with a certain person when that person yawns. Let's continue our scenario. Your reactions will vary according to the specific thoughts you have regarding the yawn, including the following:

If you thought that the yawn was meant to signify that the person was bored with you, you might feel somewhat bad about yourself. If you thought that the yawn was telling you that the other person was tired, there's a good chance that you will be indifferent. If you thought that the yawn was meant to signify that the person was bored with you, you might feel somewhat bad about yourself. If you thought that the yawn was telling you that the other person

One singular occurrence can give rise to a wide range of feelings, all of which originate in the mind of the individual experiencing them. When we are too fast to form judgments about other people without giving them the benefit of the doubt, we frequently give rise to anxious feelings. In all of your interactions with other people, you should always follow the maxim "innocent until proven guilty." If you don't, you run the risk of missing out on a wonderful romantic connection.

Utilization of Mental Replays

Cognitive behavioral therapy frequently makes use of thought recorders or diaries as a method for encouraging patients to pay appropriate attention to their thoughts and to work on ways to modify them. This is done in the hopes that the patient will eventually be motivated to change their thoughts. Although at first this could appear to be an extremely large amount of effort, as time goes on the process will become more and more second nature, and eventually the journals will not be required.

Naturally, with the introduction of mobile devices such as smartphones, tablets, and even smart watches, the process of recording one's thoughts is now simpler than it has ever been. If you always have your phone with you, you won't need to bring a diary with you anywhere else because you won't need to write anything down. On the other hand, some people believe that keeping a journal by hand helps them do it more effectively. In either case, you should go with the alternative that suits your needs and preferences the best.

CBT thought diaries are helpful not only for the individual who is keeping the diary but also for the medical experts who read it. The individual is able to read through the events that they have written down, they are able to monitor their own thinking, and they are able to identify where there is room for improvement. These diaries should be used multiple times each week following any event, no matter how mild, that causes even a moderate amount of anxiety, so that they can be of the utmost benefit to the user. The more patience you have to put into using it, the better off you will be. As soon as you feel like you're making progress in overcoming your social anxiety condition, you should start keeping a thought journal of your accomplishments. Reading through these can be just as uplifting as it can be enlightening, especially when contrasted with reading through detrimental thoughts.

Thoughts That Are Not Helpful

People who suffer from social anxiety disorder frequently struggle with two different kinds of negative thoughts. First, they will overestimate the possibility of something truly dreadful occurring, and second, they will overestimate how terrible the situation will be if that terrible event does occur. Both of these overestimations are common among people with this trait. Because of this, and because of the unhelpful beliefs, reality is twisted as a result. The person's self-perception, their perception of others, and their perception of the environment are all impacted negatively as a result of the illogical thoughts they are having. The core concept that "everyone has to like me" or "I can't ever make any mistakes" is at the center of the majority of detrimental thinking. A person will be able to discover patterns in their thoughts and will also be pointed in the direction of the underlying beliefs that are the source of their negative thoughts if they use the thought diaries on a daily basis and do so consistently. There is a good chance that you will be able to limit it down to only a handful of unwanted thoughts that are very challenging for you.

A Guide to Using Your Thought Records

When you first start using thought recordings, you might discover that it is challenging to see your way around the process of developing a more effective mode of thinking. When given enough time and practiced on a consistent basis, the new, improved thoughts will quickly become plausible to the point where they will be the first thoughts that occur to mind.

You are free to do whatever seems natural to you so long as your ideas are documented, despite the fact that many therapists will give you a form to fill out for each entry in your journal and require you to do so. The following data are the ones that need to be recorded by you:

The event that causes activation

Describe in great detail the scenario or occurrence that brought on a significant unfavorable reaction or emotion, such as anxiety or panic, and explain how it came about. It can have been anything that happened in your life, a thought that you had, a memory, or anything else at all that set off the emotion. Only the facts of the occurrence should be written down. Be sure to pay close attention to key details, such as the location where the event took place, the types of persons who were there, and the like, especially if there were any words or deeds that might have served as a trigger.

www.ingramcontent.com/pod-product-compliance
Lightning Source LLC
Chambersburg PA
CBHW011958090526
44590CB00023B/3770